Subtlety To The Simple

Edward Schwartz

iUniverse, Inc.
Bloomington

Subtlety To The Simple

iUniverse books may be ordered through booksellers or by contacting:

iUniverse
1663 Liberty Drive
Bloomington, IN 47403
www.iuniverse.com
1-800-Authors (1-800-288-4677)

ISBN: 978-1-4697-9825-7 (sc)
ISBN: 978-1-4697-9826-4 (e)

Printed in the United States of America

iUniverse rev. date:4/20/2012

For David

"The poet's eye, in a fine frenzy rolling,
Doth glance from heaven to earth, from earth to heaven,
And as imagination bodies forth,
The forms of things unknown, the poet's pen
Turns them into shape and gives to airy nothing
A local habitation and a name."

– William Shakespeare, *A Midsummer Night's Dream*,
Act V, Scene 1

BOOKS BY EDWARD SCHWARTZ

POETRY

A FOOT ON THE THROAT (Italian)
KALEIDOSCOPE
COLORS OF ETERNITY
SCHWARTZIAD
EMBRACING THE WORLD
INSIDE THE RAINBOW
THOUGHTS (Russian)
ROTATION (Russian)
SUBTLETY TO THE SIMPLE

PROSE

DREAMS COME AT TWILIGHT
THE CASE OF DONALD HUSE
DON'T THINK ABOUT TOMORROW
SEEKING THE FIREBIRD'S NEST
ONE STEP FORWARD, TWO STEPS BACKWARD
PRETEND YOU ARE HAPPY
THE GREEN SKY
RAINBOW BEHIND THE BACK
THE WHITE CLIFF
DEEP DANGER
JEWISH BLOOD
DESTRUCTION
THE GUILT

PREFACE

Poetry was always a reflection of humanity since life has begun. James Russell Lowell once defined poetry as "something that makes us better and wiser by continually revealing those types of beauty and truth that God has set in all souls."

Poet is a violin and a violinist simultaneously. Like Padre Martin, from one of the French mediaeval parables, who writes a mesa for himself and listen it, a poet also enjoys the acoustical reverberations of his poetry but, in differ from Padre Martin, he wants to share his joy with his readers.

Main themes of poetry always were, and is, philosophical meditations and love lyrics. Meditations is an attempt to understand the surrounding us world, to comprehend the world's harmony in all its manifestations – good or evil, beauty or ugliness; an attempt to comprehend harmony of the world through its disharmony. Lyric verses reflect splashes of the poet's soul, lyric poetry is always being written only by soul.

The verses made up this collection were written between 2008 and 2011 and carry a wide specter of themes – love, sense of life, faith, and many others. Open the book, my reader, and I do hope that you'll find among my verses something for your soul.

Contents

PART ONE   Meditations 1

PART TWO   Lyrics 151

Part One

MEDITATIONS

Love is a base of life,
Without love, your life is getting darker,
Sun postpones its arrival,
And shades follow you like a crazy stalker,
Be in love!

*

The world around you is perfect,
Do not try to make it better;
Your inner world is not perfect,
Try to make it better.

*

Do not justify doubts with ignorance,
Doubts lead you to the edge of decadence,
Ignorance leads you to its abyss.

Your life is a gift of Heaven,
Do not ask what for it was given,
Accept your life as a priceless treasure,
Live with dignity and pleasure.

*

Is there happiness in Paradise?
God knows,
Is there happiness in Hell?
Devil knows,
Is there happiness on the Earth?
Who knows?

Open your soul to the forest,
And you will hear the singing of birds,
Open your soul to God,
And you will hear the singing of stars.

Your sweet dreams
Rushed to the abyss of the past,
Pain of imagination
Still lives in your present,
But it is already cleaning a path to the future.
What will live in your soul in the future?

Who can say when love was born in your heart?
Who can say how long she will live?
Love is the eternal treasure,
Her age cannot be measured.

*

Having discovered "new",
You did not renovate the world.
Fool,
Your "new" is only the forgotten "old."

Passion is a base of indifference.
After the bonfire of your passion extinguished,
The subject of passion is indifferent.

*

Do not think your life is always pleasure,
Do not lose your head with love,
Do not search for the eternal treasure,
Rely on what is given from Above.

*

Wine of passion is strong,
Wine of love is stronger,
Passion does not live too long,
Love – not too much longer.

Do not forget,
The charm of past is dust,
Be afraid of traveling in the carriage of the past…

*

In our own eyes,
We are all genius –
Nobody can be compared with us;
In the eyes of others,
We are all mediocrities –
Nobody wants to be compared with us.

*

There is no future without past,
There is no progress without intellect,
There is no death without life,
There is no miracle without God…

Your wit and your body are in your custody,
But do not forget that,
Selling your wit,
You are not better than a whore selling her body.

*

You cannot correct your past,
Do not try,
You cannot see your future,
Do not try,
You cannot reach perfection,
Do not try.

Being in the chains of spiritual slavery,
You will discard them never,
Do not dream to become free,
Spiritual slavery is forever!

Life is like a shade in a sunny day –
As soon as the sun gone,
The shade vanished away…

*

Nobody knows,
Why we cannot pursue dreams,
Nobody knows,
Why we cannot see the face of beauty,
Nobody knows,
Why we cannot realize the goal of our life.

*

Why at the end of our life,
We cannot understand that
What was quite clear at the beginning?

Despite
Our wit cannot comprehend
The enigma of creation,
Our heart cannot express our admiration.

*

To doubt in everything,
or
To trust in everything –
We are given only two opportunities;
It is impossible to level them for unity.

*

We do not hear the singing of stars,
We do not hear the cry of our soul,
We do not hear the music of eternity…
Aren't we deaf?

What is good in you?
What is bad?
Do not search for the answer,
If "good" and "bad" are flowers,
You are a bucket.

For passion and indifference,
It is peculiar time,
For joy and sorrow,
It is peculiar time,
For hope and disappointment,
It is peculiar time,
For doubts and faith,
It is peculiar time.
Do we have enough time for everything?

*

If you are given conscience, human being,
It is not an award but the punishment,
Now you are sentenced to the life-long soul-digging.

Reveries come and go away,
Reserving hopes,
Love comes and goes away,
Reserving emptiness,
Life comes and goes away,
Reserving nothing…

Without wit,
You cannot reach wisdom,
Without wisdom,
You cannot comprehend God,
Without comprehension of God,
You cannot realize your wit…

The world of feelings shrinks with years.
When years are getting lazy,
The charm of past turns into dust,
And feelings of the past
Seem laughable and crazy.
Alas!

If you discarded some old sins,
You are not a man of means.
Fool, do not forget,
You are not sinless yet.

*

I asked my Angel,
Does Spirit of Life differ from Soul?
He smiled,
Spirit of Life can be given by Devil,
But Soul is being given only by God.

*

A man is great,
But he is far from perfection;
Yesterday he cried from anxiety,
Today he enjoys felicity…

Not everybody is handsome,
Not everybody is smart,
But everybody is great with the soul beauty,
Given by God…

*

You cannot go beyond your wit,
You cannot look into alien's soul,
You cannot embrace eternity,
You cannot realize the Torah's immenseness…

*

Perverting the existing world,
You will not find the soul's gold,
Good and bad cannot be equal –
Perversion is evil.

Wrinkles are tracks of your doubts,
Extinguished eyes are tracks of your doubts,
Disappointment and indifference are tracks of your
doubts,
Don't doubt, fool!

*

Temptation
is
The beginning of your destruction,
Sin
is
The end of it.

*

Give your body others,
It belongs to you,
Give your heart others,
It belongs to you,
Do not give your soul others,
Soul does not belong to you.

Only few people
Pluck up the courage to be "a white crow" in the sinful
world.
When sins are on sale,
Depravity always prevails.

*

Life offered you many temptations,
And you accepted all of them.
Fool,
You forgot God gave you the right of choice,
Relieve repentance!

*

Doubts turn your life in trash,
Do not hope you will be regained,
Like Phoenics from the ash…

Injustice cannot destroy the world;
It's only your imagination of justice,
Imagination depends on how young you are or old.

Promises are never small,
All of them are endless,
Promises are never old,
All of them are eternal.

*

Do not borrow your hopes from Devil,
Your life will be a miserable action,
Return your dreams to God,
The award will be beyond your expectation.

Everyone
Can write a book of his life on earth,
No one can write a book of his life on the heaven.

*

A man who tries to comprehend the truth,
Brings people less good
Than a man who glorifies life;
The truth is beyond comprehension.

*

Not everybody
Comes to the world to realize his vocation,
Not everybody will be blessed with the spark of
illumination.

Clever people say, "Life is a hypothesis,
Nature is its proof,"
Wise people say, "Life is the axiom,
Torah does not need the proof."

*

With every passed day
We lose our unbelief,
With every passed day
We reinforce our faith.
How many days do we need to realize the truth?

*

Do not ask God
To give you what you consider good for you,
Ask God
To give you what He considers good for you.

If mistakes of your past live in your present,
You are a fool,
If your past lives in the present of your son,
You are a sage.

Do not think about yesterday,
It has passed,
Do not think about today,
It is passing,
Do not think about tomorrow,
It will pass,
Think about the future…

From God – soul,
From Devil – soullessness,
From Man – egotism.

Time is an invention,
Do not mention it,
Enjoy your present,
Either past or future do not exist.

*

Does passion last longer than love?
Does love last longer than passion?
Do feelings defeat wit?
Does wit defeat feelings?
Who can give the answers?

*

Do not catch a word that flew off your lips –
People of few words are the best,
Do not puff up the fire of the passed passion –
The charm of the past is in the past.

Do not blame fate in your failures,
Fate is your creation.
Blame your weakness and a lack of action.

*

Not having lost,
How can you find?
Not having asked questions,
How can you receive answers?

*

How beautiful the world is –
The sky, the rains, the soil,
How beautiful you are –
Your face, your heart, your soul…

Foolishness is not joy,
Misery is not joy,
Loneliness is not joy,
The old age is not joy…

The one who is impregnated with vanity,
Gives birth lie,
The one who is impregnated with lie,
Gives birth vanity…

*

Why did we come to the world?
God knows,
What do we find and lose?
God knows,
Will our children be happy?
God knows…

Forget evil,
You cannot keep it in your heart for a long time,
Remember kindness,
It feeds your heart for a long time…

*

Truth is not born in argument,
Love is not born in difference,
Hate is not born in brotherhood,
Lie is not born in harmony.

*

In your youth,
Wine of love intoxicates you easily,
In the old age,
The more you drink the sober you are.

Enjoy your life in ripeness,
But do not forget,
Time will come to confess
In everything,
That was half-good and half-bad.

*

Tolerance in faith is meaningless.
Putting up with an idol,
You are getting godless.
Fool!

*

The world around you is perfect –
This is God's creation,
The world inside you is far from perfection –
This is your creation.

Love does not like doubtful words,
She always finds winners,
Who consider her cares the award.

*

Sediment of bitterness always lives in dreams;
What's more bitter –
The realized or not-realized dreams?

*

For a clever and for a dopey,
For a rich and for a poor,
It will be one end,
And for us, my reader,
It will be one end –
We will come to the world,
Where there is neither wit nor wealth.

Every fate depends on God,
Do not point to another one with envy,
The fate that was given you, is unique,
Every fate marked with the highest probation merely.

*

That what is being today considered recognition,
Tomorrow will be considered rejection,
That what is being today considered ingeniousness,
Tomorrow will be considered mediocrity.

*

Do not keep a bird in the cage,
Do not take a sin on your soul,
The bird has to sing on the branch,
Love has to be a human goal.

Honey and salt are given for pleasure –
Everything is from God;
And exaltation, and pain you cannot measure.

Neither prophets nor saints are around me,
I see only the sinful faces,
In the deprived world,
Love vanished without traces.

Can passion be long-term?
Can love be eternal?
Can joy be sad?
Can the old age be happy?

You cannot return the passed passion,
You are like a bird in the cage –
Your wit and feelings are not in your possession.

*

Simplicity of life is the top of perfection,
Joy of life cannot be measured,
Do not forget,
Love is a short-time pleasure.

*

If you are a human,
You do feel vibrations of your soul,
If you are a human,
You do feel alien's pain as your own.

As a bird doomed flying,
A human doomed dreaming.
When your dreams gone,
You are already a dead man.

*

I heard success has lost his way.
If he knocks at your door,
Do not drive him away…

*

I asked a friend of mine,
Do dreams die?
Looking at me,
He shook his head in clever silence;
My dog is wise,
He always gives me his advice.

The height of feelings is inconceivable,
The depth of wit is inconceivable,
The height of imagination is inconceivable,
The depth of Torah is inconceivable.

*

Charm is illusive,
Love is deceptive,
That what seemed yesterday beautiful,
Today seems laughable.
Alas!

*

Do not rely on your heart,
It is blind,
Do not rely on your wit,
It is deaf,
Rely on Torah…

Among the books on my bookshelf,
Torah lightens with hope,
My fate is in the Book of Life and Death,
On what page is it? God knows…

*

If you are clever in your eyes,
You are a dope,
If you are clever in your son's eyes,
You are a clever man.

*

Do not say that you are a pure wit,
And sins around concern you only a little bit.
If you put up with sins,
You cannot be a man of means.

Do not compete with evil,
The winner reinforces it,
Struggle with evil,
The winner kills it.

The absence of appreciation is a trouble,
The absence of vocation is the tragedy.

A sage in his eyes is a fool,
A sage in his heart is a sage.

Do not justify greediness with misery,
Do not justify weakness with the old age,
Do not justify soullessness with faithfulness.

Living in the world of hate,
Do not pray for a happy fate,
Will be the Better World full of light,
Or will it be the same eternal night?

Do not ask God for anything,
Everything is already given you,
Deserve you or not,
But God gave you the world.
Glory!

Can sin be small if it was big?
Can you look young tried on the wig?

*

Tangled in love,
Do not search the path of passion,
In passion – more sins than compassion.

*

If you bow today,
Tomorrow you will fell prone,
If you betray today,
Tomorrow you will be deeper down.

At the end of your life,
Do not consider you a sage,
The comprehension of life does not depend on age.

If you see wit far away of you,
You are a fool,
If you see wit in front of you,
You are a clever man.

If nights shrink,
Days are getting longer,
If love shrinks,
Passion is getting no longer.

Condemning, do not judge,
And judging, do not condemn,
You are only a man, not a judge.

*

If your heart is broken,
No sense to stick debris together,
The heart will look like new,
But you will regain your feelings never.

*

Why the way home seems always short,
But the way to happiness long?
Why youth is always bright,
But the old age is full of dimmed nights?

If you do not remember your past,
You did not deserve your present,
If you got accustomed to your present,
You did not deserve your future.

If you lost wealth,
You kept hope of earning more in future,
If you lost love,
You kept hope of finding another one in future,
If you lost future,
You kept no hopes.

Why do we forget that our life is our debt?
God keeps us alive
To be prepared better for the future life.
Glory!

Treating your body,
You make your soul stronger,
Treating your soul,
You make your faith stronger.

*

Do not think about tomorrow,
Every tomorrow is new,
Live today without sorrow,
Maybe tomorrow will not exist for you.

*

The age increases value:
The age of ripeness increases the value of body,
The old age increases the value of soul.

If a lie repeats itself,
It turns into the truth,
They are the same,
The difference is myth.

*

They say, "*in vina veritas*"*.
If it is,
The truth is always on the bottom of the glass.
Bottom up!

*

As there is no rain without clouds,
There is no life without doubts.
Alas!

----

* The truth is in wine (Latin)

Is there joy without laughter?
I do not know,
Is there happiness without tears?
I do not know,
Is there love without sin?
I do not know.

Do not discard your past,
It is a part of you,
Without past,
In future there will be nothing new.

*

Run away of the old age,
Be in love with young dreams,
You are neither a wizard nor a sage,
You are a man of means.

Do not blame you for the past,
It has already passed,
But do not transfer mistakes of the past
Into the present
Not to make it the past.

*

The old age without care is sheltering,
The old age without love is existence,
The old age without respect is punishment.

*

How wonderful youth is!
How beautiful joy is!
How volatile passion is!
How boring the old age is!

Stumbled over a threshold,
You are afraid of going faster,
And miss your last chance to run away of the past.

*

Wit builds life,
Stupidity destroys life,
Wisdom restores life.

*

If you are a wealthy man,
You have a lot of friends,
If your wealth gone,
You are poor and alone,
Alas!

Wit and foolishness are two sides of one coin,
Foolishness is given us to sin,
Wit is given to excuse sins.

*

Love depends on age.
In our youth,
It is love to the beauty of body,
In our old age,
It is love to the beauty of soul.

*

Life leads us to the dead end,
But knowing it,
Nobody searches another way – to the Promised Land.

Rewarding tolerance,
You reinforce evil,
Struggling with tolerance,
You reinforce good.

*

"**I** will pay for evil" is an empty phrase,
If you did not pay in no time;
To put up with evil is a crime.

*

Everything vanishes in the past –
Love and hatred, good and evil,
Only God's Revelation lives in souls of generations
forever.
Glory!

Joy of life – love and children,
Joy of death – rescue from suffering.

*

Narrowing the world in your eyes,
You will not be happy:
Even in the narrowed world,
A clever man is clever, a dope is dopey.

*

The one who is in search of good finds good,
The one who is in search of evil finds evil,
The one who searches nothing,
Cannot realize what is good and what is evil.

Spirit of sadness weakens,
Spirit of despair kills,
Spirit of faith reanimates,
Spirit of hope reinforces.

*

Foolishness is always subjective,
For someone, this is the absence of wit,
For another one, this is the height of wisdom.

*

Do not blame the Moon for the deemed light,
You cannot make it brighter,
Do not serve a beggar with gold of your soul,
When you are impoverished,
Nobody would reward you.

With years,
You are not getting better or worse,
The world is getting narrower in your eyes;
With years,
You are not getting younger or old,
The world is shrinking in your eyes.

*

Enjoy your life,
It is short to doubt,
You are not perfect?
This is not your fault.

*

You cannot move a rock with empty hands,
You cannot catch a fish in a dry riverbed,
You cannot touch a foggy dream,
You cannot hear your soul's scream,
Alas!

Sorrow ends with joy,
Joy ends with sorrow,
Birth ends with death,
Death ends with birth…

*

Where from are bones in a womb?
God knows,
Where from are thoughts in the head?
God knows.
Where from is love in the heart?
God knows,
There from are doubts in the soul?
God knows…

*

Forgot good words? Who will remind you?
For the sin of tongue, who will punish you?
From life mistakes, who will keep you?

A lot of ways are in the fuss of fuss,
But only one of them is chosen for us.
Where is it, who knows?

*

Without love,
A jiffy becomes eternity,
In love,
Eternity becomes a jiffy.

*

Do not struggle with the common sense,
You will always be a loser,
Do not pay attention to it,
You would be wiser.

Day passes and goes away,
Shade passes and goes away,
Life passes and goes away,
All passes…

Do not try to understand the future,
Not knowing the past;
If the past for you is only dust,
Between the past and future is nothing mutual.

*

In our world,
There is neither ugliness nor beauty,
In our world,
There is only difference and similarity.

Do not expect perfection in beauty,
Be smart,
Old beauty is only a pale copy of the original art.

*

Love is the light for body,
Torah is the light for soul.
Glory!

*

Do not look at the world
Through the peephole in the door,
You will see only the narrow infinity;
Open the door to the world wider,
You will see the wide eternity.

What is behind? Man knows.
What is in front? God knows…

*

Man has no power over birth,
Man has no power over death,
Man is born not for power,
Man is born to glorify life.

*

Conscience is not the award for foolishness,
Consciousness is the punishment for wit.
Alas!

Man does not know
Who he will become,
But when he became,
Who would tell him of who he has become?

*

For every time there is its doubt,
For every doubt there is its time,
For every age there is its love,
For every love there is its age,

*

Studying the Theory of Doubts,
You repeat mistakes of the past;
The theory is weak, rely on practice.

When stupidity sits on the throne,
Wit always wallows in dust,
When doubts kill faith,
In what god we trust?

*

The starting point of progress is self-confirmation,
The exiting point of progress is revelation.
What's between?

*

I roamed at twilight
Until I saw the light and read the sign,
"You missed the Promised Land,
In front of you – the dead end."

No doubts live in my soul –
The life is fuss of fuss,
But my God, how beautiful she is!

*

Being in love and admired of fate,
We cannot imagine yet that
Love maybe not the one we dreamed about,
And in our fate,
There is nothing to be proud.

*

Not everyone can fly on the wings of joy –
Sins pull us back to earth,
But if you landed off, enjoy,
Forget your fears,
Fly…

Do not lend your soul,
You will not receive her back, fool;
Foolishness creates soullessness.

*

On the threshold of eternity,
Do not consider yourself soulless,
If you gave your soul children,
Your life was full of sense.

*

Do not put the guilt for sin
Only on yourself,
For you,
It's enough a half.

Joy of life is not what
You feel in your heart,
Joy of life is what
You feel in hearts of your children.

Nobody can embrace the world
That is immense,
Nobody can recover the sight in blindness,
Nobody can catch the firebird of happiness,
Alas!

*

Share the diamonds of knowledge with others
Before the bonfire of your doubts arises;
After all,
Diamonds will turn into ash,
The wealth of knowledge will turn into trash.

How many sad days were in your life?
Who counts!
How many joyful days will be in your life?
God knows…

*

We studied the science of love for all our life.
But the science was difficult for us –
We remained ignoramus,
Alas!

*

Your life is a shade in a sunny day,
Enjoy your life and pray:
Life lasts no longer than a jiffy of love.

Do not remember your sins,
Mistakes of the past
Give birth the fear of future.

*

Remembering youth,
Enjoy your life in ripeness,
Remembering ripeness,
Glorify God.

*

Every sunrise and sunset is a miracle,
Enjoy your life but do not forget,
Your life is God's present.
Glory!

If you do not want to get old,
Do not make mistakes of the old age
In your youth,
If you want to remain young,
Repeat mistakes of your youth,
In your old age.

In the fuss of ordinary – beauty,
See it!
In the beauty of fuss – ordinary,
Discard it!
In tears of youth – happiness,
See it!
In tears of old age – despair,
Discard it!

*

Being in love with life,
You are a short of breath,
Life is always sinful,
What is sinless? Alas, only death.

How I am weak in my body!
How I am strong in my faith!

*

Who is a man?
An observer of the world;
For everything he sees,
He cannot stop glorifying God.

*

Being afraid of discarding doubts,
I carry them with me.
But, not discarded them,
Shall I be able to reach my life's acme?

My Lord,
You have presented me the world.
Please tell me who am I?
What is my destiny and why?

*

They say, I am strange,
And full of sinful thoughts,
But I am only trying to discard my doubts
About what is beyond the bound?

*

On the threshold of eternity,
Everybody sees the light,
On the threshold of eternity,
Man is perfect, world is bright.

$$T$$ears of rain
Give birth to the beauty of life.
Without tears
Can soul be alive?

*

$$W$$hat is life? This is the beginning of the end.
What is death? This is the end of the beginning.

*

$$W$$it cannot explain inspiration,
Wit cannot explain God's creation,
What is wit?
This is only the self-proclamation.

When love becomes habitual,
When your hairs become gray,
When only narcotics create hope,
Then nightmares prevail over your dreams…

*

Your life is a chain of foggy days,
Enjoy your life,
But be afraid of God, and pray.

*

Life is provisional,
Sin is forever,
Life dies,
Sin – never.

Searching for the sense of life,
You will never reach your goal,
Life is the fuss of fuss,
It has no sense at all.
Alas!

*

Do not envy to your happy friend,
Happiness is subjective,
What today you consider happiness,
Tomorrow will not seem you attractive.

*

If you are full of life,
You have to realize,
God well-disposed to you,
And always gives you His advice.
Glory!

Struggling with yourself,
You kill your "ego".
Are you a winner or a loser?

*

The fingers of my hands were not enough to count my
sins.
I was confused,
To count sins – this is not an amusement.

*

If you lost your "I" in the crowd,
Do not try to find it,
This is not a matter of being bad or good,
This is a matter to be or not to be proud.

Foolishness is given us by God
To minimize frustration
For not understanding the world;
Do not blame your foolishness,
Nobody understands that what is beyond our
understanding.

With passing years,
Life is going upside down,
The one who seemed to be in his youth the king,
In his old age seems to be a clown.

Everything goes to the end:
Joy – to tears,
Feelings – to indifference,
Beauty – to ugliness,
Love – to suffering,
Life goes to death.

To love or not to love?
That is not a question.
What and whom?
That is the question.

*

The more love medicine you take,
The more the bonfire of love blazes up.
What's the sense of treatment?

*

Do not try to find oblivion in beauty,
What beauty is?
What you considered beauty yesterday,
It seems you ugly today.

Yesterday – a cry of joy,
Today – a pre-death groan,
Life is short, enjoy every day.

*

Do not turn your doubts over,
They are eternal.
Enjoy your life, fool,
You are not immortal.

*

Bowing in waist,
You lower your spirit,
Rising to the height of spirit,
You extend the bounds of the world.

If you do not doubt,
The world is beautiful,
If you doubt – vice versa,
Do not doubt, fool,
Wit is always controversial.

I asked my Angel,
What is the difference between wisdom and foolishness?
He smiled,
The difference is in the level of stupidity…

What is life?
Temptations of sins,
What is life?
Prayers for success,
What is life?
Confessions in sins,
What is life?
Prayers for the painless death.

And wise people feel tiredness,
Not knowing,
Who would inherit their wisdom?

*

Life for me is the award,
Every sunset and sunrise is a miracle,
How can I find words to glorify God,
Who presented me the world?

*

I asked my Angel,
What is it, infinity?
He smiled,
This is only a composition of eternities.

To be a poet is a wonderful occupation,
But only God knows whether
Poetry is your vocation.

Joy finishes with tears,
Sadness finishes with tears,
Life finishes with tears.
Alas!

Do not discard joys of life,
The world is full of them,
Discard your weaknesses,
You are full of them.

I asked my Angel,
Is there treatment from love?
He smiled,
Love is only the fever of the body,
Take cold shower.

*

Our life is the fuss of fuss,
Beauty is an illusion,
How can we be happy and avoid confusion?

*

In the sinful world,
Confessions do not relieve sins,
But make them habitual.

Hope is charming,
Dream is beautiful,
Do not grumble that life is awful!

*

Hopes feed youth,
Dreams ennoble adolescence,
Remembering consoles the old age.

*

Do not put alien's sins on your shoulders,
For you,
It is quite enough to carry the burden of your own sins.

If you are young,
You want to accelerate the present
To see the future;
If you are old,
You want to stop the present
Not to think about the future.

*

"Nothing" is a part of "something."
What is nothing?
This is the measure of everything.

*

Wit and stupidity are given us from God,
Wit is the punishment,
Stupidity is the award.

Mystery of death cannot be solved
By the knowledge of life,
This is an enigma, unsolved while you are alive.

*

The way of life is defined in advance:
For someone is to remain unknown,
For another one is to be in great demand.

*

When your soul is full of doubts,
Your youth leaves you,
When your soul is empty,
Your life leaves you…

What is the fuss of fuss?
This is the search of youth,
What is the fuss of fuss?
This is the search of wisdom,
What is the fuss of fuss?
This is the search of truth.

*

Do not look at alien's eyes,
You will see the alien's imagination about you;
Do not look at the mirror,
You will see your own imagination about you,
Look into your soul…

*

If love is a part of the past,
Why does she live in the present?
If the past is a part of eternity,
Why eternity has no past?

I asked my Angel, why in the youth
There are a lot of questions,
And we always know all answers?
Why in the old age,
There are only few questions,
But we never find the answers?
He smiled,
Questions are from man, answers – from God.

If your soul sings,
You are in harmony with the world,
If your soul cries,
You are in harmony with yourself,
If your soul keeps silence,
You are already dead.

Your love is a cry of blood,
Your love is a smoke of booze,
Can it be called "love" if it was not given by God?

For your sins,
Do not search a scapegoat,
For your sins,
Ask for forgiveness;
You cannot run away of yourself,
Do not persuade yourself you are sinless.

*

What is self-expression?
Sometimes – sacrificing,
Sometimes – self-denying,
Sometimes – self-burning.

*

Everything what you see,
Have already seen,
Everything what you hear,
Have already heard,
Everything what you talk about,
Have already talked,
Everything what you have talked about,
Have already seen,
Alas!

All of us are given criteria:
From God – criteria of faith,
From Devil – criteria of fault.

*

I asked my Angel,
Where do doubts lead to?
He smiled,
In science, they lead to discoveries,
In faith, they lead to soullessness.

*

Live with love human,
Sing songs of admiration,
And die with love on your lips,
Glorifying God for His Creation.

How rapidly youth passes,
How rapidly thoughts get grey,
How rapidly life passes away…

It is terrible to live in blindness,
It is more terrible to live in the fuss of fuss,
It is horrible to live in uselessness,
It is more horrible to live in desperateness.

*

Sometimes,
An enemy is dead but hatred is alive,
Sometimes,
A friend is alive but friendship is dead,
Sometimes
We live feeling neither friendship nor hatred.

Comprehending wisdom,
You cannot reach soul's perfection.
Perfection is unreachable like the enigma of Creation.

*

Do not tell "love is dead,
And life has gone."
Fool,
If your dreams are alive,
Your life is going on.

*

Time will pardon nobody,
Neither you nor me,
Life is short,
Hurry up to reach acme.

You cannot ran away of your fate,
Do not try,
You cannot avoid putrefaction,
Do not cry…

Turning over the pages of the Book of Life,
I did not find in it the cut ones;
I prostrated to anybody,
And lived in accordance with my conscience,
Glory!

*

There is no fume without fire,
There is no hatred without love,
There is no death without birth,
There is no faith without God.

Capricious wind disperses clouds on the sky,
Cleaning the way for stars;
Fool,
Do not console yourself
That future is the forgotten past.

*

I asked my Angel,
Is there spirit in the wit?
He smiled,
Edward, if not, who leads it?

*

Happiness is God's gift,
It comes to people which await it.
Be happy!

I asked my Angel,
Do I differ from others if I'm full of sins?
He smiled, Edward,
The difference is in your prayers and verses.

Do not complain to God,
That your wit is trite,
You cannot change it for the new,
Your wit does not depend on you.

*

The past has memory,
But does not have a face,
The present has a face,
But does not have memory,
The future
Has neither a face nor memory.

Singing of birds is God's voice,
Rustle of leaves is God's voice,
Noise of surf is God's voice,
Cry of soul is God's voice,
Glory!

Do not search respect if you did not deserve it,
Do not search wisdom in foolish thoughts,
Do not search the sense of life in the fuss of fuss,
Search God in your soul...

*

Listening wise people,
You increase knowledge,
Listening fool people,
You lose time.

Do not expect
Your son will be like you,
Do not expect
Your son will be better than you,
Expect,
Your son will be different from you.
How much different? It depends only on you…

*

Do not have pity on the lost opportunities,
Have pity on the lost life…

*

Do not be a sage in your eyes,
This way leads you to stupidity,
Praise wisdom since your youth,
In the old age, wisdom will praise you.

God created you genius,
Put in your head myriads of neurons.
How can you use them?
Aimlessly – studying the laws of love,
Wisely – studying the Laws of God.

Keep your wit healthy,
Heart – opened,
Soul – pure,
Thoughts – clear.

If your dreams extinguished,
And your heart is full of emptiness,
Do not invite love to the empty house.

Whirlpool of delight carries away fool people,
Whirlpool of glory carries away haughty people,
Whirlpool of indifference carries away satiated people,
Whirlpool of life carries away all...

*

Do not boast with your victories,
Did you defeat your ego?
Do not boast with your achievements,
Did you reach your goal?
Do not boast, fool...

*

I asked my Angel,
Why do some people
Build the Temple of Soul,
But others guard Divine Bones?
Edward, he said, everyone has his goal.

Love is the endless passion;
If you feel your love is restricted,
Hurry up to a confession.

Everything is on sale,
Hurry up to buy or sell,
But do not forget,
Sold your soul,
You will forever be in debt.

*

If you do not think about your soul,
Soul does not live in you,
If you think about nothing,
Nothing lives in you.
Are you still alive, fool?

Blaming your fate in your fouls,
Do not expect to receive the new,
The Book of Fate cannot be rewritten by you.

*

Do not call an idiot a man,
Who considers two by two is equal five.
In his world,
There is the different beginning point.

*

A road to nowhere is a bumpy road,
Do not hurry to reach the dead end,
There is no way backward.

We realize the necessity to change ourselves,
Only after we have already changed,
Alas!

*

The world is not restricted with dimensions,
Try to understand it, fool,
If there are four dimensions,
There are also and five – this is a rule.

*

Where is the beginning of the end?
God knows,
Where is the end of the beginning?
God knows,
Where does the road of your life lead to?
God knows…

Passion burns soul,
And turns darkness into light,
But if you live without soul,
Can your passion be bright?

*

Jiffy is jiffy,
It's unrepeatable,
If love gone,
She is irretrievable.

*

Do not tell that you are unfaithful.
If you discarded God in your soul,
You are already dead, fool…

Future is a forgotten past,
Present – strange and foggy,
Is there reality in present?

*

There are no doubts without sadness,
There is no sadness without doubts,
There are no dreams without hopes,
There are no hopes without dreams…

*

Life experience comes with years,
Love experience – never comes.

It is easy to sell,
It is easy to betray,
It is not easy to vindicate,
It is difficult to forgive.

*

Take care of your heart,
This is the source of body,
Take care of your soul,
This is the source of your spirit,
Take care of your faith,
This is the source of your life.

*

There is love that covers sins,
But there are no sins that cover love.

Earning wealth,
You sell your soul to the slavery of avarice;
Trying to set her free,
You will pay everything you have earned.
What is your profit, fool?

Do not rely on your friends,
You will remain alone,
Do not rely on your children,
You will remain not understood,
Do not rely on yourself,
You will remain disappointed.

*

Faith, Hope and Love create God's symphony,
All other sounds create only cacophony.

It is easier to put up with stupidity,
Than to contest wit,
It is easier to go downstairs,
Than to lift up,
It is easier to sin than to confess in sins.

Do not put yourself in the epicenter of the human hive.
There is no movement here,
But without movement, there is no life.

*

Chain of life is short:
Yesterday – glory,
Today – indifference,
Tomorrow – oblivion.

Without faith,
Life is punishment:
Sunrises turn into sunsets,
Friends turn into the enemies.

*

I asked my Angel,
Who am I, nobody or somebody?
If nobody,
Why I was sent to the world?
If somebody,
Why I did not become an idol?
He smiled,
Edward, you are everybody…

*

Do not ask Life
For everything you want to have;
She will give you
Only what she wants to give.

A man who is chosen to see the world,
Stands stock-still from admiration,
Trying to find words how to glorify God for His
creation.

If a man is good,
Why fear, envy and meanness live in him?
If a man is bad,
Why faith, soul and love live in him?

Reason warns,
Wit saves,
Wisdom rescues.

Wit gives an advice,
Wisdom carries the truth,
Stupidity shows the way to Power.

Selling your body,
You will lose more than acquire,
Selling faith,
You will lose everything.

*

Sorrow has the beginning and the end,
Happiness has neither the end nor the beginning,
Why do we consider
The end of sorrow is the beginning of happiness?

To be an apostate in science,
It is sometimes justifiable;
To be an apostate in faith,
It is always punishable.

*

And the "chicken blindness" – blindness,
And the small fuss – fuss,
And the pale beauty – beauty,
And the broken dream – dream.

*

Wrinkles tell you about the passed years,
Radiance of eyes – about the dreams…

I asked my Angel,
What is the charm of love?
He smiled,
Edward, she lives only in the present,
And dies if present turns into the past or the future.
Alas!

If in your ripeness
You did not read respect in your son's eyes,
In your old age,
You will read in them indifference.

*

The field flowers will die,
The green grass will become grey,
The blue sky will become black,
That day
When nobody will remember
God's name on the Earth…

The road of benign intentions leads to Hell.
The less we ask God for us,
The more He gives us consolations.

*

What is the sense of creation?
God knows,
What is the sense of destruction?
Devil knows.

*

Your life is only a jiffy,
Hurry up to realize it,
Your life is God's creation,
Hurry up to justify it.

Doubts are the award for stupidity,
Doubts are the punishments for wit,
Let's leave doubts to ignoramus.

*

Rain and sun – this is joy of life,
Love and hatred – this is joy of life,
Doubts and disappointments – this is joy of life,
Birth and death – this is joy of life.
Glory!

*

I asked my Angel,
What is the charm of the old age?
He smiled,
Edward, the charm is in prayers for sins of the youth.

You are only ash,
Do not be naive,
If today you are something,
Tomorrow – nothing,
Hurry up to live.

*

If success is easy,
Life does not seem difficult,
If success is difficult,
Life does not seem easy.

*

Do not be dopey,
Life is a miracle.
Not understanding it,
You are getting miserable.

Do not justify sins with tolerance,
Tolerance is weakness,
It destroys human's base.

*

Moral is a lady without a face,
For some of us, she is perfect,
For others – full of defects.

*

I asked my Angel,
What is the sense of life?
He smiled,
Edward, the only sense is love.

The world of feelings is a volatile world,
Today – love, tomorrow – hatred,
Today – you are young, tomorrow – old.

*

Do not seek a happy fate in the world of hate.
Love and hate are syllogisms,
Happiness – is atavism.

*

If light in your soul extinguished,
The world around you changed –
You became soulless,
Soullessness does not depend on age.

To understand what life is,
Open Torah,
To realize what happiness is,
Open Torah,
To comprehend what the truth is,
Open Torah.

*

I asked my Angel,
What does it mean, "To live in vain"?
He smiled,
It means, not found the way to God.

*

I roamed in darkness for many years,
Until I heard the voice, –
Your life is your choice.

Love is a fever of body,
The only medicine is time,
Do not hurry up to be recovered,
You will become another guy.

Keeping love in your heart,
Do not forget the rules of storage:
Love does not endure lie,
She keeps freshness despite her age.

*

Hard worker-wind drives clouds on the sky,
He blow – and they are near my threshold,
My thoughts are also like clouds,
But their direction depends on God…

My self-portrait got me upset,
I saw an unknown man:
His face was young but mine is old,
His heart is hot but mine is cold.

*

I asked my Angel,
Where can I find my love?
He smiled, Edward, don't seek,
She is always being given from Above.

*

Going up,
A choice of way is yours,
Going down,
You do not have any choice, –
The way is one.

Why beauty is never clever?
Why dopey is never happy?
Why Devil is full of evil?
Who knows!

Colors of love prevail in dreams,
Colors of fear prevail in nightmares.
What colors? God knows.

If the sense of your life is love,
You are a youngster,
If the sense of your life is disbelief,
You are a blind,
If the sense of your life is a prayer,
You are a wizard.

If you did not forgive,
And was not forgiven,
You lived your life in vain.
Alas!

*

When your life is done,
You will never be cloned
To receive the new one,

*

If neither love nor compassion
Lives in your soul,
Neither cries of orgy nor cries of exaltation
Create harmony in your soul.

Foolish thoughts live in my mind:
If I am old,
Why the world is so bright?

*

Do not forget your father's lessons, son.
When he gone,
Nobody would give you advice,
What is bad and what is nice,
Alas!

*

Do not hurry along the road of knowledge,
In haste, you will know nothing,
Do not hurry to gain life experience,
You will gain it, advancing in years.
Live with pleasure,
Pleasure will make your knowledge wider,
And experience deeper.

On the bonfire of your desires,
You cannot prepare the soul's meal.
Extinguish it. Until you satisfied desires,
Your life is full of material.

*

Mirage of future is always far away of you.
Approaching it,
You see that future is a forgotten past.
Alas, in future there is nothing new...

*

Two by two is equal four, –
You did not get accustomed to doubt.
If you think the result is different,
Do not express your thought
Not to be laughed at.

Your memory is powerless,
You cannot restore the past.
Do not try, the past is dust.

*

Beauty and ugliness are both subjective,
There is nothing to be done.
While your mind is an active sense,
It always creates beauty from ugliness.

*

Love life and beauty,
Live and die with love,
Love is a present from Above,
Glory!

When you are young,
Love is gold,
When you are old,
Love is mold.
(If you are very old)

An avaricious man forgets debts,
A generous man forgives debts,
A clever man does not make debts.

*

What a crazy life is in the human hive!
You have to struggle with yourself
To feel you are alive.

Remembrances of the past are always full of sadness.
Your youth was full of love,
Ripeness – craziness.
Was your life full of happiness?

What is life?
A jiffy of love,
What is love?
A jiffy of life…

Do not search for your soul
Behind the fence of indifference;
Fool,
This is the house of soullessness.

The warehouse of memory keeps mistakes of the past.
But rummaging about them,
Do not search your passed love,
The past is dust.

*

Youth lives with passion,
The old age lives with indifference.
What is the stimulus of life in ripeness?

*

Advancing with years,
We are not getting clever,
Advancing with years,
We are not getting wiser,
Advancing with years,
We are getting older and sillier.

If you do not see the world is getting new,
It means that something wrong's with you,
Your soul is getting rough,
You do not feel somebody's pain and laugh.

A straight road of life,
And a curved one
Lead you to the same dead end.
There is no way out...

Do not hide a face of stupidity
Under the mask of arrogance, –
You cannot wear a mask for life.

In the crazy world,
Bad and good merged together.
Do not try to separate them, fool,
This is the useless work, the work forever.

*

If you feel the taste of life,
Do not be afraid of being crazy,
Love!

*

Sons of sons are the crown of age,
They are your profit and your gain,
They are your hope that
You lived not in vain.
Glory!

If man contrives God,
He contrives himself.

*

I asked my Angel,
How much past is in the past?
How much present is in the present?
How much future is in the future?
He smiled,
Edward, these are all jiffies.

*

Going up along the staircase,
Leading down,
You stay on the same level – the level of stupidity.

Do not dissolve wine of love
With water of indifference;
On the bottom of the glass,
You will find sediment of bitterness.

*

Composing capricious jiffies,
You will receive the number of the passed years.
Is this an equivalent of volatile happiness?

*

Sins are on sale,
Hurry up to buy,
In the sinful world,
There is no soul's gold.

How much is two by two?
This is not an enigma,
In the world we have built,
Common sense is a dogma.

*

Bowing waist at the young age,
You will not be able to straighten in the old age.

*

Sin is a harbinger of repentance,
Pride – destruction,
Haughtiness – fall.

You can get accustomed to good and evil,
You can get accustomed to love and hatred,
You can get accustomed to life and death.
Can you get accustomed to desperateness?

*

To penetrate into the enigma of thoughts,
This is a dream,
To touch the dust of eternity,
This is a dream,
To understand God's creation,
This is a dream.
Dream and you will be happy.

*

Trying to get to know your fate,
You lose time;
Fate was forecasted from Above,
This is an enigma of the human hive.

I asked my Angel,
Can I see the light of Eternity?
He smiled,
Edward, it is visible only through
The debris of your soul…

*

Since the date of birth
To the date of death,
You try to change yourself.
Fool, you are powerless,
Your weak points are endless.

*

A man who goes out of the temple is always better
Than a man who comes in.
Hurry up to become better!

Do not find reasons
Why you are not a holly man;
You are a human,
Try to be a man of means.

*

A thread of reason and consequences is very thin.
But do not try,
To pull it through the needle of your sin,
This is impossible!

*

I asked my Angel,
Who am I?
He smiled,
Edward, you are a naive but faithful guy.

Your life is written on your forehead.
If you are not afraid of the truth,
Look at the mirror and read…

*

Do not look at the world
From the height of your years, –
You will see nothing;
Look at the world
From the height of your soul, –
You will see everything.

*

Entering the world,
We are sinless,
Advancing with years,
We are advancing with sins,
And ask God for forgiveness…

All of us – the revolted slavers of the senseless ideas,
Our fate is clear, our life is done,
Discarded one idea,
We shall be chained forever to another one.
Alas!

At first glance,
All of us look the same,
Although some are proud of themselves,
Others – good for nothing trash.
When we turn into ash,
At last glance,
We shall again look the same.

*

If a man lived a thousand years,
Nobody would find
A trace of his life on the earth,
If a saint lived a thousand years,
Nobody would find
A trace of his life on the heaven,
Alas!

God's creation is a sample,
Only a wizard knows it,
Who is a wizard?
He is the perfect wit.

*

Do not preach idiots with your dogmas.
If they discarded your dogmas,
Their wit is wiser than yours.

*

I asked my Angel,
How old is Beauty?
He smiled,
Edward, she is young as Eternity.

Do not find the mistakes of the past
In the present, –
Your life will turn into nightmare;
The charm of the past is in the past,
This is the eternal truth, be aware.

Wisdom is a bride of Truth,
Wisdom is a sister of Wit,
Wisdom is a mother of Faith.

Our arrival and departure
Do not depend on us,
But our life is in our power –
We can live with hatred or with love.

Do not postpone your life for tomorrow,
Live today,
Tomorrow may be full of sorrow.

*

When dreams are broken,
Your eyes are full of tears.
Do not cry, fool,
Even broken dreams are a part of happiness.

*

If son's wit doubts in his father's wisdom,
Can father be proud of his son's wit?

Do not destroy the spiritual house of your father,
You will inherit wind,
And only got old, you will understand
What wealth you lost because of your stupidity.

*

World is a walker-wind,
World is a drunkard-rain,
World is an amorous cloud,
World is a fairy tale written by God.
Glory!

*

Standing on the threshold of my home,
I observed rotation of the sky.
If behind the threshold is eternity,
Where am I?

Our world is full of suffering and negation,
Our world is full of disappointments,
"Another world" is full of contemplation and alleviation,
But it stripped of love and hope.
What world is "the better world"?

*

Looking at skies for God's advice,
We forgot
That God is inside us.
Glory!

*

They say "the world is full of fools",
But all evaluations are subjective,
To look smarter and more attractive,
Nobody wears a badge of foolishness.

I asked my Angel,
Is there the beginning of the end?
He smiled, Edward,
There is only the end of the beginning…

*

Discard your years,
But put yourself together,
You will feel much younger,
But will not be a young man ever.

*

The price of good and bad
Depends on time,
What we consider priceless in youth,
In ripeness it doesn't cost a dime.

Do not keep sadness in your heart,
It makes you weaker, older,
Discard it,
You will be younger, bolder.

*

My watches are without hands,
But they are running good.
Where do they lead me?
Forward to Hell or backward to my childhood?

*

An hour of your departure
Does not depend on you,
Until you see a crack on the sky,
Each day is wonderful and new.

The enigma of death
Does not differ from the enigma of life,
Life and death are God's conception.

*

The essence of God we cannot realize,
The essence of God is beyond comprehension,
Nobody can measure the Galaxy size
Or witness the devils' invasion.

*

Life in the human hive is the struggle with time.
Kill time if you want to be alive.

Do not think about tomorrow,
Tomorrow will take care of itself,
Drink the wine of your life today,
Live with zest, enjoy…
Bottom up!

*

The dissolution of flash is punishable.
Became an animal,
You lost your human's soul.

*

"Bad" and "good' is semantic of words.
In devil's world,
There are devil's laws.

The fuss of sinful thoughts broke my sleep;
The charm of the past has passed,
Don't try to return it.

*

Do not carry the burden of sins,
This is not a treasure;
You are going to the world,
In which neither love nor sins are measured.

*

Separating "you" and "your ego",
You reinforce your soul,
Separating "good' and "bad",
You reinforce the world.

I asked my Angel,
How can I improve the world?
He smiled,
Edward, improve yourself,
Donate your soul's gold.

*

From unfaithfulness to God,
It seems to be not far away,
But if you lost your road,
You will spend lifetime in vain.
Alas!

*

The less you know the better you sleep,
What for do you adore your wit?

Surrogate love can abuse you,
Surrogate love can seduce you,
Surrogate love can kill you,
But she cannot absorb you.

*

I asked my Angel,
Why do people trust in false gods?
He only shrugged…

*

Knowledge is force
But it cannot defeat blind stupidity;
In the world of absurd,
There are different plans of reality.

I asked my Angel,
Where does Beauty live?
He smiled,
Edward, she lives in every soul,
Do not be naive…

*

What is his vocation?
Man does not know,
What is his devotion?
Man knows…

*

Two-faced morality is not an exception:
One is for dreams, another one – for reality.
Do not be surprised, fool,
Such morality is a man-made creation.

I asked my Angel,
If a poet did not become in great demand,
What was the sense of his life and art?
He smiled,
Edward, who knows? Only God…

Do not try to understand the world, fool!
This is the axiom of creation,
Nobody is chosen to comprehend that
What is beyond comprehension.
Alas!

*

A man who perceived desperate in his soul,
Did not become weaker; he became darker,
A man who perceived joy in his soul,
Did not become stronger; he became brighter.

Compromise gives birth to "relative truth,"
Does it differ from "relative lie" if both of them are
relatives?

I asked my Angel,
What does it mean "to live with zest?"
He smiled,
Edward, it's simple,
Try to be the best.

*

God created us for purposes,
Sages – for thanksgiving services,
Poets created to write verses.

If in our blindness,
We call the bright light darkness,
What is the difference between wit and foolishness?

*

Can a little good change a lot of bad?
Can a little bad change a lot of good?
Can anything change something?

*

Condemning the world,
You maybe young or old,
But you are always wrong –
The world is perfect,
You are not.

My gloomy thoughts dispelled like clouds,
The world is beautiful1.
While your dreams are alive,
Enjoy your life,
Discard your doubts, fool!

*

On the fist of life, meal is plentiful.
You will miss a zest trying to taste it all.
If you want to be alive, fool!

*

Nights follow days – this is death and birth rotation,
Discard your sadness,
Death is only a part of your reincarnation.

I asked my Angel,
The world will die with me,
or
I will die with the world?
He smiled,
Edward, the world will die *only for you*.

*

Do not call glory happiness.
Happiness is the absence of craziness.

*

Your face is not a mirror's reflection.
Being your soul's reflection,
It reflects the soullessness of your generation.

Dreams gone like water through sand,
Life is only an instant,
Somewhere there is the Promised Land,
But Life is not enough to reach it.
Alas!

*

Do not dream of becoming immortal,
Immortality – is a fairy tale;
Sold Devil your soul,
You will be forever imprisoned in Hell.

*

Do not hurry up to say,
"I am done."
You are alive –
It means your life is going on.

How many years do we need to realize,
That the world will die
Not with us but for us?

*

Today you are sinful,
Tomorrow you are sinless,
Today you are pious,
Tomorrow you are godless.
Who are you?
You are God's creation, Devil's correction.

*

When I think about the world
That God gave me,
My soul sings.
The only thought makes me unhappy –
I could not find words to glorify God.
Glory!

I have advanced in years
And gained a lot of past.
Alas,
My gain turned out dust…

*

Do not invent "philosophical stone"
To become rich,
Gold – is not the universal treasure;
If gold in your hands has price,
The price of your soul's gold cannot be measured.

*

The law of life is very tough:
To reach acme, you must be genius,
Your talent is not enough,
Alas!

Who can predict tomorrow,
Not known what past was?
Who can feel today's gladness,
Not felt what sorrow was?

When you are young,
Love is the only treasure for you;
When you are old,
Health is the only treasure for you.
What does it mean "the only treasure"?
The answer depends on point of view…

*

Reaping dignity,
Expect to sow respect,
Reaping bows,
Expect to sow contempt.

Part Two

LYRICS

I AM FULL OF YOU

All my dreams are full of you,
Sweet dreams!
All my thoughts are full of you,
Crazy thoughts!
All my hopes are full of you,
Endless hopes!
All my desires are full of you,
Painful desires!
I am full of you…

MUSIC OF YOUR NAME

Music of your name sounds for me
Like a firebird's singing,
Music of your name sounds for me
Like a mantra,
Music of your name sounds for me
Like a prayer,
Music of your name sounds for me
Like Music of Life…

THE AGE OF LOVE

You wear my mother's name, –
How old are you?
You look like my daughter, –
How old are you?
When you embrace me,
I feel like a kid, –
How old are you?
You are old like Eternity,
You are young like a newborn day,
You – my love; what is the age of love?

I FELL IN LOVE WITH YOUTH

I fell in love with youth,
But flowers laughed at me,
Fool, she loves her dream, not you.
I fell in love with youth,
But trees laughed at me,
Fool, she loves to be admired by you,
I fell in love with youth,
But rain cried on me,
Fool, she loves your poetry, not you…

AMALGAM OF DARKNESS

Amalgam of darkness, where are you,
Amalgam of darkness, I love you…
In darkness,
Foolishness does not seem awful,
In darkness,
Dreams do always seem colorful,
In darkness,
Friendship is always trustful,
In darkness,
Love is always beautiful.
Amalgam of darkness,
Cover me by your wing,
Amalgam of darkness,
Turn my heart's winter into spring.

PICTURE OF LOVE

Your eyes are bottomless,
Your lips are plump,
Your hairs are soft,
Your skin is tender,
Your face is beautiful, –
From what fairy tale did you come to me?

BONFIRE OF MY SOUL

I threw into the bonfire of my soul
All my hopes,
I threw into the bonfire of my soul
All my rhymes,
I threw into the bonfire of my soul
All my life,
And the bonfire of my soul lighted up the world of
dreams.
Tender white clouds smiled at me,
A firebird waved me with her wing,
And love covered me by her tender veil…
Only death can extinguish the bonfire of my soul.

ETERNITY

I kneeled in front of you,
And your murderous beauty made me speechless,
The words of love stuck in my throat.
I looked into the abyss of your eyes,
And everything mixed up in my mind –
Stars on the dark sky,
And flashing stars of my conscience,
Waves of hope and waves of the ocean,
Remembrances of the past, and dreams about future…
Have I seen the Eternity of Love in your eyes?

WHAT FOR?

Meeting you, this is the suffering for me,
What for?
Meeting you, this is the punishment for me,
What for?
Meeting you, this is a gift for me,
What for?
Meeting you, this is an award for me,
What for?
Meeting you, this is a new life for me,
What for?

FOOL!

I met you,
And heard a whisper of roofs,
Fool,
Love is not your goal.
I met you,
And heard a cry of rain,
Fool,
Love is a torch of your soul,
I met you,
And heard a laughter of clouds,
Fool,
Love is your foul.
While I kept silent, you left.
Roofs do not whisper,
Rain does not cry,
Clouds do not laugh,
Silence is profound.
Fool!

GOD KNOWS

How long do dreams last?
God knows,
How long do hopes last?
God knows,
How long does love last?
God knows,
How long does happiness last?
God knows,
Why did God send you me?
God knows.

A PROMPTER

I whispered "I love you",
And you repeated my words.
How happy I was
To be in love with goddess!
I whispered the words of love again,
But you corrected me,
No, you mixed the pages,
Here I have to hear the sounds of rain.
What could I say?
You were an actress-premier,
But I, alas, was only a prompter.

YOUR LOVE IS DEAD

When trees do not chat to flowers,
When beauty does not differ from ugliness,
When every new day
Looks like yesterday's,
When your tears
Dry like a drop of rain in the sun's rays,
Your love is dead.
Do not try to reanimate it –
The charm of the past is in the past.

KEEP SILENT

Do not tell me "no."
While you keep silent,
I hope,
And my hope keeps me alive.
I write you my verses to express my love,
But my lips also keep silent –
The silence of souls is the acme of love.

WHERE ARE YOU?

My day today is upside down,
I feel like a king who lost his crown.
Ugly faces hurt my eyes,
Faces of deception, envy and lies.
The sun dies on the sky,
Hiding between clouds,
The world is in darkness, without bounds.
Drops of heavy rain fell on my palm,
Damaging thoughts, corrugating realm…
Where are you, my love?

THE FIREBIRD'S SONG

I looked at you,
And your eyes opened for me the door into the New
World.
I came in and saw magnificent flowers
That smelled with hope,
I saw the trees of wonderful imagination,
And firebirds that sat on every branch.
It is so easy to catch them, I thought,
Why do people think the firebird is one?
At that moment I saw a girl gathering flowers.
What is your name? I asked her.
Love, she said, smiling.
No, I smiled in return as I recognized the girl,
Your name is Sarah.
That is right, she agreed, Sarah means love.
One of the firebirds sat on Sarah's shoulder.
Sweaty, she said, sing us a song.
What song? The firebird asked.
The song of love, Sarah said,
And the bird began singing.
With the first sounds of the song, my eyes closed,
And I lost myself among my dreams.
When I opened my eyes,
The sun vanished in the abyss of clouds,
And a merry-go-round of ugly faces began its rotation
around me.
You left me…

DO NOT LOVE ME

Do not love me, enough is enough,
I am not worth your love,
We live in the different worlds,
You – in the world of reality,
I live in the world of words.
We failed to reach acme,
Alas!
Do not love me,
Be happy at last.

THE BUCKET OF STARS

To warm your soul with my love,
I gathered stars from the sky in the bucket of hope,
But the stars that seemed warm,
Turned out colder than ice.
The bucket of stars fell to pieces…

COLD HEART

When I fell in love with you,
Our hearts were so close,
That I felt the heat of your heart.
When your love gone,
Our hearts were still close,
But I did not feel the heat of your heart any more.
When you left me,
Carrying the heat of my heart,
My heart became cold.
Will it be hot again?

NEGATION

Your eyes shine with the fire of passion,
Your thin fingers tremble from desire,
But on your lips, I read negation.
Humid diamonds of your eyes
Lead me to a trap of hope,
And my heart breaks off from love,
Negating your negation…

BEAUTIFUL FLOWERS

I brought you a bucket of flowers.
Where did you collect such beautiful flowers?
You asked.
In my dreams,
I answered.
Where do your dreams live?
You asked,
I was at a loss, –
Can my dreams about future
Live in the abyss of the past?

I LOVE YOU

I should like to be turned into your dreams,
But dreams are too volatile
To live in your heart for a long time,
I should like to be turned into a caged bird
To sing a song of love to you,
But who will give you the cage?
I love you.
What can I tell you more?
I am ready to pay for the arrival of the late spring
By my soul's pain,
But how long will the spring last?

MY HEART

It was cold winter,
But my heart was hot with love,
And the melted snow mixed on my eyelashes
With tears of happiness.
How a wonderful season winter is!
It was hot summer,
But my heart was cold,
Love did not warm it any more,
And the drops of rain mixed on my eyelashes
With tears of disappointment.
What a sad season summer is!

YOUR IMAGE

You were my spring,
But spring, alas, is not forever.
Dark clouds covered the sky,
And rainy days washed hope away
As if she existed never.
Bloody tears of autumn finally
Turned my dreams into delirium,
And your image vanished
In the dark abyss of my memory…

DOUBTS

I kissed you,
Sacrificing my dreams to your love,
But what it gave me?
Only doubts –
Your life remained for me
Like a distant star among the constellation of clouds.
Alas,
Your love couldn't change my life…

WEAKNESS

The words of love are a justification of my weakness.
You were eager to hear them again,
And I couldn't stop talking,
But we both know,
The words are only the words –
A jiffy of love disappeared, left aloofness in our hearts.
Why do we continue torching each other?

MY GOD!

My God!
I exclaimed, seen your beauty.
God's name flew away off my breast,
Like a firebird,
And, blinded by your beauty,
I closed my eyes.
When I opened them again,
You disappeared.
My God!
Why did you open the cage of my dreams?

TWO FACES

It was long ago,
When I wore the face God gave me...
I brought you my hopes,
And intended to tell you how bright they were,
But you burst out laughing at me and left...
I brought you my dreams,
And intended to tell you how beautiful they were,
But you burst out laughing at me and left...
I brought you my love,
And intended to tell you how tremendous it was,
But you burst out laughing at me and left...
Years passed and I met you
When I wore a face Life gave me.
Do you remember, I asked,
I brought you my hopes?
Yes, your hopes were bright;
Do you remember, I asked,
I brought you my dreams?
Yes, your dreams were beautiful;
Do you remember, I asked,
I brought you my love?
Yes, the words of love were unforgettable.
Why did you get laughing at me and leave?
Because you wore the face God gave you,
But I liked faces Life gives.
Can you love me now when I wear a face Life gave me?
I asked, but she smiled sadly,
Your sins reflected on your face,
But I love faces God gives people...

FOREVER

I'll live in sun's rays,
 – Forever!
I'll live in night rains,
 – Forever!
I'll live in your eyes,
 – Forever!
I'll live in your tears,
 – Forever!
I'll live in the singing of birds,
 – Forever!
I'll live in my words,
 – Forever!
I'll live in the world,
 – Forever!

THE WINGS

When I was young,
I built the Wings of Hope,
In an attempt to reach the Mountain of Hope,
But the wings turned out too small, –
I couldn't land off.
When I reached ripeness,
I built the Wings of Happiness,
In an attempt to reach the Mountain of Happiness,
But the wings turned out too heavy, –
I couldn't land off.
When I got old,
I built the Wings of Dreams,
In an attempt to reach the Mountain of Dreams,
But the wings turned out too light,
And I rushed into the Abyss of Eternity...

CONDEMNATION

In your eyes – expectation,
But the words of love die on my lips.
In response to my silence,
I read in your eyes condemnation, –
Fool, you are losing your happiness…
Why did I keep silent? It was beyond me,
Maybe I wasn't sure you were my happiness,
And we should be able to reach acme?

WHAT IS BEYOND?

Sunrise – sunset,
Duration of day is short,
What is beyond?
You came – you left,
Duration of love is short,
What is beyond?
Birth – death,
Duration of life is short,
What is beyond?

WHY?

Words of love are a shaky bridge
Across the abyss of feelings.
Why do we always go across it,
Knowing that most of us fall into the abyss,
And never reach happiness?

IN THE SEARCH

Remembrances go away like a thunderstorm,
The charm of past is in the past.
If you are in search for happiness,
You seem to be happy,
But if your search is over,
A rare drop of happy tears vanishes, –
Happiness turns into disappointment.
The thunderstorm of love has gone…

WHERE ARE YOU?

It is rain.
Roofs dream about happiness,
Whispering the words of love to Street Lights,
And my heart is also full of love in the expectation of
meting you.
How rapidly time passes!
You did not come,
And even the noise of rain does not interrupt
The piercing silence of my loneliness.
Where are you?

THE THUNDERSTORM

Your first kiss was like summer.
Since that day
The brass of my lips was red-hot from passion.
But suddenly the thunderstorm burst out,
The Indian ink flew on your eyelashes,
Your eyes lost its charm,
Hot lips became cold like winter,
And the cold breath of indifference froze my heart.

IMPRESSION

Rain drops like milk from the overripe breast,
The illusive image of happiness
Either appears or diminishes in front of my eyes,
Sleepy twilight creeps to the house,
And your beautiful eyes surrender to the passion
mercy…

THE FALSEHOOD

I drink bitterness of the autumn sky
And rumbling rain,
I drink bitterness of tired evenings,
And crazy nights,
I drink bitterness of the grey old age,
And crying rhymes,
I drink bitterness of the wet-painted mists,
And volatile shades,
I drink bitterness of the indifferent mercy,
And a short-time passion,
And clouds stand on end –
I feel your love was a falsehood…

WHY?

Why a human heart is so light,
So glamorous and so bright,
When we are young and anxious to start?
Why a human heart is so heavy,
So indifferent and so flabby,
When we are tired of age,
And our life cannot be changed?

INDIAN SUMMER

Sonorous silence floods fields,
The purple sun turns from the ardent monster
Into the small, tender animal,
Sunrise looks like a rare ancient coin,
And it seems the golden color prevails
On the palette of Eternal Artist.
Perfection reaches acme,
Creating the illusion
That Indian summer of love would also last forever.

MASTERPIECE

Autumn – is more black than an evening,
Days are shorter than a sleep,
The sky is black,
Roofs are full of holes,
Leaves fall off, stripping the crown of trees…
In front of me,
There is a blank sheet of white paper,
Verses die inside my soul,
Their lifeless bodies put on the paper,
Creating the masterpiece painted in white color on the
white paper.

O, TIME!

O, Time,
Do not touch me with your envy!
The drunken air still drives me crazy,
And I do not feel approaching of the dark chaos.
O, Time,
The pendulum of my thoughts still swings stable,
The Past does not worry me with its sins,
The Present creates the Harmony of Indifference,
The Future is illusive like morning clouds…
O, Time,
Do not touch me!

ABOUT THE AUTHOR

A Russia-born American writer Edward Schwartz (Dr. Eli Besprozvany) is the author of more than twenty books written in a wide literary diapason – from poetry and short stories to large-scale novels. Educated in Art, Engineering and Physics, he graduated from the College of Naval Architecture of St. Petersburg University and worked as an engineer, researcher, university professor. His books were published in Italy, Germany, Israel, the USA. He currently resides with his family in Forest Hills, New York.

You can meet him, visiting his website edwardschwartz. com